A Practical Guide to
RIDING & PONY CARE

Christopher Rawson, Joanna Spector and Elizabeth Polling

Consultant and contributor: Patricia Smyly

Illustrated by Eric Rowe and Fred'k. St.Ward
Designed by Bob Scott

Contents

2	Getting to Know a Pony	18	Paces
4	Saddles and Bridles	20	Aids
6	A Pony of Your Own	22	Changing Pace
8	Keeping a Pony at Grass	24	Changing Direction
10	Stables and Feeding	26	Learning to Jump
12	Grooming	28	Rules for the Road
13	Health	29	Country Code
14	At the Blacksmith	30	Popular Breeds of Ponies
16	In the Saddle	32	Index

Getting to Know a Pony

Learning to ride is great fun but there is much more to it than just sitting in a saddle. If you find out about horses and ponies and how to handle them, you will learn to ride well and happily.

Ponies are gentle but strong and should be handled quietly and firmly. They are startled by sudden noises and movements, so talk to a pony before you go up to him or touch him. Then he will get to know your voice and trust you.

1 Catching a Pony

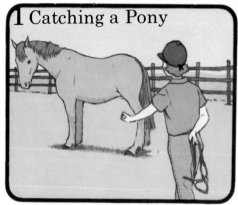

Go into the field, taking his headcollar and a titbit, such as a sliced carrot. Remember to close the gate behind you. If a pony lives on his own, give him a call.

2

If he is with others, keep the titbit in your pocket and walk him, talking quietly. Offer the carrot from your left hand as y slip the lead rope over his hea

Measuring a Pony

Height is measured in hands from the ground to the top of your pony's withers. One hand equals 4 ins or about 10 cms. Take off one centimetre for his shoes.

Face Markings

Star

Snip

Blaze

Stripe

Points of a Horse

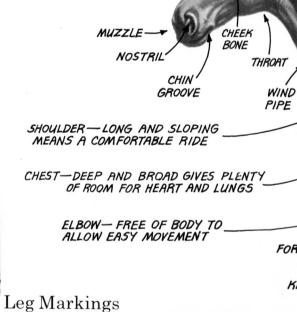

POLL

EAR

NECK—LONGER ON TOP THAN UNDERNEATH FOR GOOD BALANCE

FORELOCK

A BIG KIND EYE USUALLY MEANS A GENTLE HONEST NATURE

WITHERS—NOT TOO FLAT OR THE SADDLE WILL SLIP

MUZZLE

CHEEK BONE

NOSTRIL

THROAT

CHIN GROOVE

WIND PIPE

SHOULDER—LONG AND SLOPING MEANS A COMFORTABLE RIDE

CHEST—DEEP AND BROAD GIVES PLENTY OF ROOM FOR HEART AND LUNGS

ELBOW—FREE OF BODY TO ALLOW EASY MOVEMENT

RI

FOREARM

OFF FOR. LEG

KNEE

NEAR FORE LEG

A SHORT CANNON BONE IS STRONG

FETLOCK

E

CORONET BAND

HOO HARD STRO

Leg Markings

Sock

Stocking

2

...ile he is munching, put on the ...dcollar. Give him a pat and ...ther titbit to reward him for ...ng caught or he may not want ...ome to you next time.

Take the rope like this. Say "Walk on" and move forward. You should be able to walk at a pony's shoulder. Practise leading him from both sides.

Never do this. Most ponies dislike being stared in the face and pull back. You can teach a pony to walk forward by tapping his side gently with a stick as you move.

Horse and Pony Colours

BACK— SHORT AND STRONG TO CARRY YOUR WEIGHT

LOINS

FLANK

CROUP

HIP

DOCK

THIGH

...EATH

STIFLE

POINT OF HOCK

CHESTNUT

OFF HIND LEG

NEAR HIND LEG

...STERN—LONG ...D SLOPING TO ...ACT LIKE A ...OCK-ABSORBER

HEEL

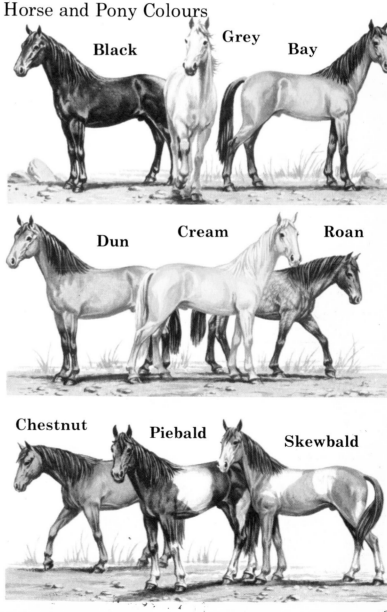

Black Grey Bay

Dun Cream Roan

Chestnut Piebald Skewbald

3

Saddles and Bridles

Saddles and bridles and other pieces of pony equipment are called tack. Tacks cost a lot but if you look after it well it will last for many years. Always try on new or secondhand tack if you are buying, as a pony will never be happy if it does not fit.

A saddle should fit without touching a pony's spine when your weight is on it. But check that it is not so high that the saddle is perched on his back. If it is, it will roll about and unbalance you both. It should not be too tight over his withers, nor too long over his loins. A general-purpose saddle you can use for riding and jumping, and a snaffle bridle, are probably the best to choose.

Keep the saddle on a bracket or saddle horse, and the bridle hanging by the headpiece. Store them in a dry place when you are not using them. Never leave a pony untied wearing his saddle as he may roll on it and damage it.

Parts of the Saddle

POMMEL

WAIST

SEAT—A SADDLE WITH A DEEP SEAT IS MORE COMFORTABLE THAN A FLAT ONE

CAN... OR B... OF T... SADD...

THE SIZE OF THE SADDLE IS MEASURED FROM THIS STUD TO THE CANTLE

THE LINING I... USUALLY MA... OF LEATHER

STIRRUP BARS ARE MADE OF FORGED STEEL. KEEP THE SAFETY BARS DOWN WHEN YOU RIDE

RUN THE STIRRUPS UP THE LEATHERS LIKE THIS WHEN YOU ARE NOT USING THE SADDLE.

STIRRUP LEATHERS—CHECK TH... REGULARLY FOR CRACKS AND SIGNS OF WEAR

SADDLE FLAP

HOLLOW CHANNEL, OR GULLET, WH... KEEPS THE RIDER'S WEIGHT OFF TH... PONY'S SPINE

UNDERSIDE OF FLAP. KEEP IT SOFT WITH SADDLE SOAP

GIRTH STRAPS MUST BE KEPT IN GOOD CONDITION

KNEE ROLL

←THIGH ROLL

BUCKLE GUARDS STOP GIRTH BUCKLES DAMAGING THE FLAP

THE FRAME OR TREE IS USUALLY MADE OF BEECH WOOD

Looking after Your Saddle

Clean your saddle after every ride. Take off the girth and stirrups. Damp-sponge off the dirt. Dry the leather, then rub in saddle soap. Polish the stirrups and clean the girth. Lastly, put everything bac... in place. If the saddle is new, it is a good idea to oil it to make it more supple. Every year have i... checked by a saddler.

Saddling Up

1 Tie up your pony. Smooth the hair on his back, then put on the saddle, like this, from the nearside. Keep the front of the saddle well forward over his withers.

2 Slide it back into place. Go to the offside and let down the girth, checking that the flap and buckles are not caught or twisted. Return to the nearside and do up the girth.

3 Tighten the girth gently, gradually smoothing the hair and skin under it. Some ponies puff themselves out, so check the girth again before and after you get on.

Removing a Sadd...

Run the stirrups up the leathers. Undo the girt... on the nearside, then li... off the saddle on to you... left arm. Pick up the girth as it comes off and lay it across the saddle.

Girths

girth is a belt which is buckled
und your pony to keep the saddle
place. Good ones are made of
lon, string or leather which
ust be kept soft.

A Jumping Saddle

ese usually have very light trees
they weigh as little as possible.
ey also have flaps shaped like
is to help keep you in the right
sition for jumping.

Parts of a Bridle

HEADPIECE — THE CHEEK PIECES
BUCKLE ONTO THIS AND ALLOW
THE LENGTH OF THE BRIDLE
TO BE ALTERED

THROAT LASH

BROWBAND
THIS STOPS THE
HEADPIECE FROM
SLIPPING BACK.

THE CHEEK PIECES
MUST BE LEVEL ON
EACH SIDE AND
HOLD THE BIT INTO
THE CORNERS OF
THE MOUTH

A PLAIN
CAVESSON
NOSE
BAND

A GOOD WIDTH FOR
REINS IS 1·5 cm. DO
NOT USE VERY LONG
REINS OR YOU MAY
CATCH YOUR FEET
IN THEM.

A RUBBER SNAFFLE BIT IS
VERY MILD. IT IS USED TO
GUIDE AND STOP YOUR PONY.
THINNER MOUTHPIECES ARE
MORE SEVERE

Looking after Your Bridle

Wash the bit after your ride so
food and saliva do not dry on it.
To clean the bridle, undo all the
buckles and wipe each piece
separately. Dry it with a chamois
leather, then rub in saddle soap
with an almost dry sponge. Put it
together again ready to use.

Types of Bits

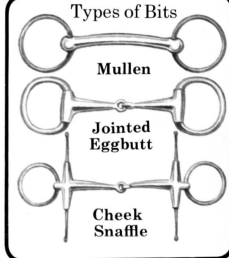

Mullen

**Jointed
Eggbutt**

**Cheek
Snaffle**

itting a Bridle

p the reins over his
ad, then, holding the
idle like this, open his
uth with your thumb.
ntly push in the bit. At
e same time, lift the
adpiece over his ears.

2

Straighten his mane and
lift his forelock over the
browband. Check that the
bit hangs level across the
top of his tongue and up
against his lips without
wrinkling them.

3

Do up the noseband and
throatlash. Your hand
should fit under the
throatlash, like this. Put
all the straps neatly in
their keepers so they will
not flap about.

Removing a Bridle

Undo the noseband and
throatlash. Lift the
reins and headpiece
gently over his ears, like
this. Allow him to drop
the bit from his mouth
as you pull off the bridle.

A Pony of Your Own

Everyone who likes riding dreams of having their own pony. Choosing one is great fun, but takes a lot of time and has to be done carefully.

Before you buy a pony, get as much experience as you can. This will help you to know what you are looking for and choose the right one.

You also need to learn how t feed a pony, catch him in a field, groom him, and put on his saddle and bridle before y look after your own.

1 What a Pony Needs

It is cheaper for you, and better for your pony, if he lives out in a field. There should be at least one acre of good grazing for each pony in the field.

2

The pony will need a saddle, bridle and a headcollar. Unless you take over the tack belonging to the pony you buy, ask your saddler to come and fit the new tack correctly.

3

In winter some ponies kept out grass need a New Zealand rug. also need extra food then. Find out if your local feed merchant can sell you hay and pony nuts.

4

5

Every four to six weeks, the blacksmith should take off your pony's shoes, trim his feet and replace the worn shoes with new ones. This takes about an hour.

6

Your pony should be treated for worms every eight to ten weeks to keep him healthy. Once a year the vet should inject him against 'flu and tetanus and check his health.

7

Here are some of the things you need for grooming your pony. It a good idea to get them before y buy a pony. If you look after the they will last a very long time.

Choosing the Right Size

It is better to buy a pony that is a little too big for you at first. Then you can still ride him as you grow older. But he should not be so big you cannot control him. If your pony is too small, you will not be comfortable and he may not be able to carry you for long. If you want to ride in competitions, make sure your pony's height is not over the class limit.

Pony Too Big

Pony T Small

e more you know about a pony
ore you buy it, the better. Look
one whose owner has outgrown
r one you already know,
haps from a local riding school.
ke someone with you who knows
t about horses.

Do not buy at an auction as you
cannot ride the ponies. Choose a
pony that is between 6 and 14 years
old and has been fully schooled.
See him in a field. Is he friendly
and easy to catch? Have him
saddled and ridden. Then ride him.

If he seems to like being ridden
and walks quietly in noisy traffic,
ask a good horse vet to check
that he is healthy. If all is well and
you are sure this is the pony you
want, then you can go ahead and
buy him.

Enjoying a Pony

u will enjoy riding on an
linary steady pony. You can also
npete in many events at local
mkhanas and Pony Club rallies.
nies usually enjoy hunting and
nping natural fences, such as

logs and ditches. Most can learn
quite easily to jump a course of
show jumps up to about one metre
high. But highly-trained show
jumpers are very expensive. They
need courage to tackle big jumps

and so may be too excitable to be
good first ponies. Showing classes
are like beauty contests—ponies
must look good and move well.

Keeping a Pony at Grass

Ponies are happier living with others, so try to share your field with a friend who has one too. Make sure they have food, water and shelter.

Your field should be fenced with post and rails, strong hedges or plain wire. Be careful with barbed wire as it can easily injure a pony. Wire should be pulled very tight with the bottom strand at least 46 cm high.

Ponies like to eat short juicy grass. They do not like the long coarse grass where droppings have fallen.

If you do not look after your field, it may become "horse sick". This means that the parts which ponies eat are bare, and other parts are covered in long, useless grass. Ponies get worms if they eat the eggs of worms which live in droppings. It is a good idea to clear up droppings regularly. It helps to let cows graze the field and eat the long grass.

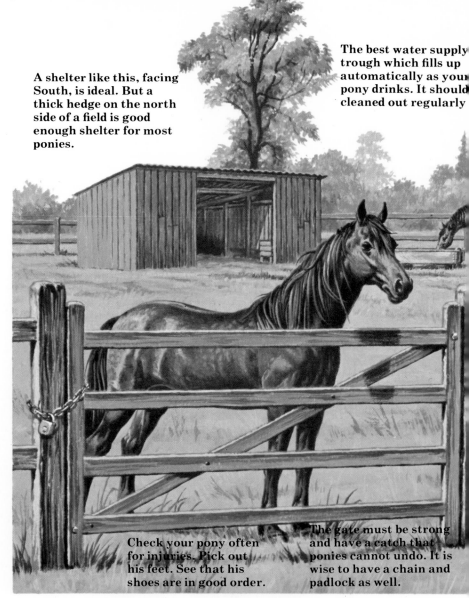

A shelter like this, facing South, is ideal. But a thick hedge on the north side of a field is good enough shelter for most ponies.

The best water supply trough which fills up automatically as your pony drinks. It should cleaned out regularly

Check your pony often for injuries. Pick out his feet. See that his shoes are in good order.

The gate must be strong and have a catch that ponies cannot undo. It is wise to have a chain and padlock as well.

1 Extra Feeding

Your pony will need hay when grass is scarce and has little goodness in it. This is usually from October to May. Putting it in a hay net hitched up high, like this, saves waste. He will need between $2\frac{1}{2}$ and 5 kilos a day, depending on his size. Always feed hay which has a sweet smell. Mouldy hay could make your pony ill or damage his breathing.

2

Ponies that look well when fed on hay alone, may n need anything else. But if your pony is working hard he will need extra food, such as nuts. They are easy to use but expensive. Feed from about 1 kilo to very small pony up to 3 kilos to a 14 hand pony, spli into 2 small feeds. Read about other sorts of food on the next two pages.

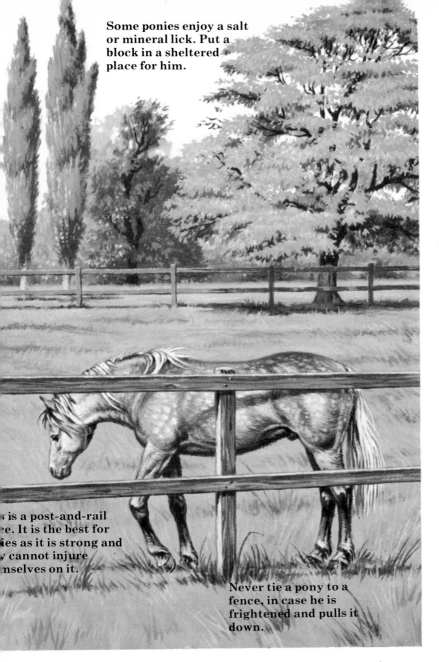

Some ponies enjoy a salt or mineral lick. Put a block in a sheltered place for him.

...s is a post-and-rail ...e. It is the best for ...es as it is strong and ... cannot injure ...nselves on it.

Never tie a pony to a fence, in case he is frightened and pulls it down.

Poisonous Plants

BRYONY

RAGWORT

YEW

LABURNUM

RHODODENDRON

DEADLY NIGHTSHADE

FOXGLOVE

CHERRY LAUREL

PRIVET

HEMLOCK

Search your field and hedges for poisonous plants before putting your pony in. Uproot any you find and burn them. Put a fence round any harmful shrubs or trees to keep them out of reach. Too many acorns are poisonous but most ponies do not eat them.

Grooming

...ush off dry mud with a dandy ...ush, but do not brush too much ...this will remove the natural ...ease which keeps your pony dry ...d warm. Tidy his mane and tail, ...nge his eyes, nose and dock and ...k out his feet.

Cold Weather

Your pony can stay outside even in weather like this, as long as he has extra food to keep him warm. Give him at least as much as a stabled pony. When it freezes, do not forget to break the ice on his water trough every day.

A New Zealand Rug

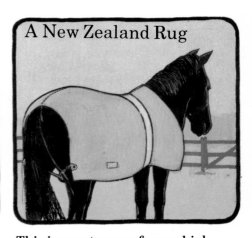

This is a waterproof rug which your pony can wear during the winter, if he is part-clipped or if he does not grow a thick coat. Make sure it fits correctly and check it every day or it may begin to rub and make him sore.

Stables and Feeding

If you ride a lot and your pony needs to be really fit, it is best to keep him stabled. Clip his thick winter coat so he does not sweat and lose weight, and keep him warm with a rug.

There is no need to keep him in all the time. A few hours a day in the field will keep him happy and easy to manage. Try to stick to a regular routine, such as this, which suits you and your pony: 7.30 am—Give water, a feed, a small haynet and muck out. 10.00 am—Brush your pony, pick out his feet, exercise for least an hour. 12.00—Small f and turn out till tea time. 4.00 pm—Groom thoroughly bed down. About 5.00 pm— Fill water bucket, and hayne give evening feed. Before yo to bed check all is well.

The Stable

A loose box, like this, with a divided door is ideal. A strong shed can often be used. It should be at least 3 x 4 metres, with a high roof and a doorway 1.20 metres wide. Rough concrete, to stop him slipping, makes a good floor. It should slope down slightly towa the drain.

Feeding

Ponies have small stomachs for their size so they need to eat little and often. The basic food that replaces grass for stabled ponies is hay, which is a bulk food. They also need other sorts of food to give them energy. All ponies need different amounts.

Good hay should have a sweet smell, and be crisp to feel. Never feed musty or mouldy hay, nor hay that is less than six months old. Give less energy food if you cannot exercise your pony. Be sure he has water to drink before each feed.

Energy Foods

These are the most important part of a hard working pony's diet. They make him strong and fit and ready to work.

Oats

These can make ponie hot and excitable, so fe only small amounts, w crushed, to begin with They should be clean, at least six months old

Barley

This is a good fattening food but not so heating as oats. Feed it well crushed or boil whole grains for 2-3 hours.

Maize

This is not so full of protein as oats but sho still only be fed in very small quantities.

Looking after the Stable

ver the floor with deep bedding
keep your pony comfortable and
rm. Wheat straw is best, except
a greedy pony who may eat it
d get too fat or even ill. Peat,
od shavings, sawdust or
redded paper are also good.

Muck out each morning. Remove
the droppings and wet straw. Stack
the clean straw in a corner and
brush the floor. Re-lay the bed,
banking it round the walls. Add
clean straw when it is needed,
which may not be every day.

Tools You Will Need

Buy good tools that you can handle
easily. Use a basket or skep to
carry droppings from the stable.
You will also need a broom, a
shovel and at least one fork. Do
not use a fork with sharp prongs
as this could be dangerous.

Rugging Up

2

3

jute rug is usually put on a
pped pony at night, in winter,
th one or two underblankets. In
ytime, a woollen rug is useful
side, and a New Zealand rug for
tside. Throw it on like this.

Make sure it is well forward. Then
do up the front buckle. From the
back, pull the rug into place.
Walk round to the off side to make
sure that the rug is hanging evenly
and is not caught up.

Put on the roller and do it up tight
enough to keep the rug in place.
Smooth out any creases. To take
off the rug, remove the roller, undo
the front buckle and slide it off
backwards.

ulk Foods

ese are parts of your
ny's diet which help
fill him up. They also
op him eating the
ergy food too quickly.

gar Beet Pulp

is must be soaked for
hours before feeding.

Chaff

This is hay which has been
put through a chaff
cutter. This should be
done little and often or
chaff will become dusty.

Bran

Bran is a useful bulk food.
It is the ground outer
husks of wheat. It can be
fed dry with oats or damp
in a mash. Warm bran
mash is good for sick
ponies.

Nuts

There are lots of different
sorts of pony nuts. Mostly
they are a ready-made
mixture of energy and
bulk food which gives
your pony the same
balanced diet all the time.
There are other sorts,
called low-protein nuts
which are mainly dried
grass. They are all easy to
store and feed. Some
fresh greenery or
vegetables each day will
help his digestion.

Grooming

There are two kinds of grooming. They are brushing to remove mud and make the pony look tidy; and deep grooming which cleans and massages the skin and helps to keep your pony fit and healthy. If your pony lives at grass, use only a dandy brush, or you will remove the waterproof grease from his coat. Pick out his feet before you ride. If your pony is stabled, deep groom him every day after your ride. Then the pores of his skin are open and the scurf loose.

1 Speak quietly, then run your hand down the leg from shoulder to fetlock and pick up the foot. Use the hoof pick from heel to toe to get anything that is lodged there.

2 Slide your hand down the back of the lower leg and lift the hind foot in the same way. Clean out the foot like this, taking care not to hurt the sensitive frog.

3 Brush off mud and sweat stains with a dandy brush. This has hard bristles and will also bring scurf to the surface. Use short, firm strokes except in tender parts.

4 Deep groom with a body brush, using short circular strokes with your weight behind the brush. Clean the brush with the curry comb after every few strokes.

5 **6** Carefully wipe round his eyes and nostrils with a damp sponge, or cotton wool which you throw aw Clean under his tail using anothe sponge kept just for this job.

7 Put the mane on the wrong side, then brush it back into place, a few hairs at a time. Brush the tail like this, with a body brush. Take care not to break any hairs.

8 Put a coat of hoof oil on the hoof wall. Put it also on the sole and frog if you have washed and dried them. This looks good and helps to stop them cracking.

9 Use a damp water brush to lay th mane and untidy hairs at the top of the tail. Lastly, wipe your pony all over with a clean cloth so his coat is smooth and shiny.

ealth

st ponies are tough. If you
e good care and feed them
sibly, they will probably
ealthy. But illness and
dents can happen, so learn
t to look for and when to
the vet. A healthy pony
a shiny coat, bright eyes
eats well. Look out for
s of lameness, poor
etite or a dull coat. Notice
is losing weight or putting
oo much. Start your own
t Aid kit with cotton
l, wound powder, antiseptic
ment and bandages.

Coughs and Colds

If your pony starts coughing, keep
him alone so he does not infect
others. Send for the vet. Colds
last about 10 days, but your pony
must be rested for several weeks.

Keep him warm and offer tasty
food, such as warm damp mashes
with glycerine, honey or treacle
to soothe his throat. Cut out hard
food. Rest a pony with a cough.

olic

s is a tummy pain and is
etimes due to bad feeding. It
y be very serious. Call the vet
nediately and keep your pony
m and moving until he comes.

Laminitis

Ponies which eat too rich grass
sometimes suffer from this.
Tender parts in the front feet swell
and become so sore it hurts them
to walk. Call the vet.

Worms

Different kinds of worms can live
inside your pony, eat his food and
get into his bloodstream. They
will make him thin and unhealthy
if he is not treated regularly.

uts

the small cuts in mild antiseptic
warm water. Dry the cut and
on wound powder. Deep cuts
y need stitching by the vet
the pony kept in and rested.

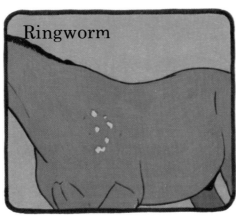

Ringworm

Small, round, bare patches appear
anywhere on the body. It is very
catching, so isolate him and handle
in rubber gloves. Ask your vet for
something to help clear it up.

Cracked Heels

Wet pastures or too much washing
can give your pony sore heels. Try
to keep them clean and dry, and
ask your vet for a suitable healing
cream.

At the Blacksmith

Horses which run wild do nct need shoes. Their hooves wear down naturally. But horses which work or travel on hard roads need their feet protected by metal shoes. The hard outside of the horse's hoof grows about 5 mm each month. This needs to be trimmed or the horse may go lame. To do this, the blacksmith takes off the old shoe, cuts off the extra growth, and fits a new shoe.

An electric fan behind the forge blows air into the fire to make it hotter.

The blacksmith cuts long pieces of fullered iron into short lengths to make horseshoes.

Water to cool horseshoes.

Blacksmiths wear leather aprons to protect their clothes from wear and sparks.

This blacksmith is hammering a red hot shoe into shape.

1 Shoeing a Horse

First the blacksmith uses the sharp edge of a buffer to loosen the nails which are holding the old shoe on to the horse's hoof.

2

Then he levers off the old shoe with pincers, taking care not to twist it sideways or damage the outside wall of the hoof.

3

He uses clippers, called hoof parers, to cut away the extra wall which has grown since the last time the horse was shod.

4

To make quite sure tha both sides are level an that the new shoe will comfortably, the blacksmith rasps the h

Being a blacksmith is a very difficult job to learn. Young men, called apprentices, train for many years before they are good enough to make and fit horseshoes on their own.

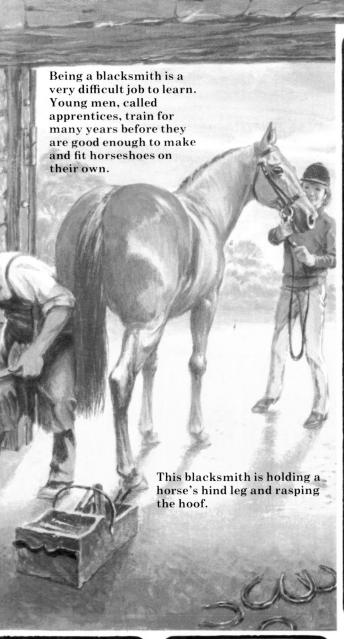

This blacksmith is holding a horse's hind leg and rasping the hoof.

Parts of a Horse's Hoof

CORONARY BAND

HORNY WALL OF HOOF

HEEL

TOE

WALL

WHITE LINE

SOLE

THE FROG IS MADE OF RUBBERY HORN IT ACTS LIKE A CUSHION AND STOPS THE HOOF SLIPPING

Parts of a Horseshoe

A GROOVE CALLED FULLERING RUNS ROUND UNDERNEATH THE SHOE

NAIL HOLES

CLIPS

NAIL

THIS IS A HORSESHOE FOR A HIND FOOT. IT HAS CLIPS ON EACH SIDE TO HELP HOLD IT ON. HORSESHOES FOR FRONT FEET HAVE ONLY ONE CLIP ON THE TOE

...resses the hot shoe ...o the hoof to make ...e it fits exactly. The ...l of the hoof has no ...ng so it does not hurt.

6

Now the blacksmith nails on the new shoe so that the points of the nails stick out about 3 cm up the wall of the hoof.

7

When the points of the nails have been twisted off, he hammers them from underneath, holding pincers under the ends.

8

Finally he rasps the outside of the hoof and the points of the nails, called clenches, so there are no sharp edges.

In the Saddle

Always remember to wear a hard hat whenever you go riding. Before you mount your pony, make sure that the girth is tight enough or your saddle may slip round. Try to sit with your knees and thighs close against the saddle, ready to grip and keep you steady. Once you learn to do this, you will not be tempted to use the reins to keep your balance.

YOUR BACK SHOULD BE STRAIGHT BUT NOT STIFF.

KEEP YOUR SHOULDERS WELL BACK AND YOUR ELBOWS CLOSE TO YOUR SIDES

KEEP YOUR AND LOOK AHE

KEEP YO HANDS JU ABOVE TH WITHERS

SIT IN THE MIDDLE OF THE LOWEST PART OF THE SADDLE

YOUR KNEES AND ANKLES ACT LIKE SPRINGS. TRY TO KEEP THEM SUPPLE

REST THE BALL OF YOUR FOOT ON THE STIRRUP

KEEP YOUR HEELS DOWN

Tightening Your Girth

Move your leg forward and lift the saddle flap. Pull up the straps one at a time, pushing the spike of the buckle into the higher hole.

Mounting

1

Stand beside your pony's near shoulder, facing his tail. Hold the reins in your left hand with a handful of mane, like this. Hold the stirrup with the other hand and put the ball of your left foot into the stirrup iron.

2

Spring up as lightly as possible, taking care not to jab your pony's side with your left foot. Hold either the front or back of the saddle with your right hand.

3

As you straighten your left knee, swing your right leg up off the ground and clear over your pony rump. Take care not to touch hi with your foot on the way over.

Holding the Reins

Holding the Reins

Your hands are the most important link between you and your pony. Hold the reins lightly so you can just feel your pony's mouth. From the bit, the reins should pass between your third and little fingers, across the palms of your hands and be held between your thumbs and first fingers.

Keep your hands level, one on each side of your pony's neck about 10 cms apart. Hold the reins with your knuckles facing the front and your thumbs on top like this.

OLD THE REINS SO YOU
KE A STRAIGHT LINE FROM
UR ELBOWS TO THE BIT

Adjusting Your Stirrups

Dismounting

1

up the loose end of the stirrup
her, holding one finger on the
e of the buckle. Now you can
e the leather up or down
out losing the end.

Take both feet out of the stirrups so your legs are hanging free. Now lean slightly forward and, still holding the reins, rest your left hand on the pony's mane.

With your right hand on the front of the saddle, lean slightly forward. Then swing your right leg backwards and clear over your pony's loins.

3

4

down gently into the saddle so
do not hurt or frighten your
y. Put your right foot into the
rup iron and take up the reins
oth hands.

Slide gently down, well away from your pony's front legs. Remember it is dangerous to dismount by swinging your right leg forward over your pony's neck.

Run up the stirrup irons and take the reins over your pony's head. To lead, hold the end of the reins in your left hand and both reins close to the bit with your right.

Paces

Ponies have four paces—walk, trot, canter and gallop. Learn to ride them correctly, then you and your pony will be comfortable and will work happily together.

Walking

The walk is the easiest pace because it is calm and steady. You have time to think about the right way to ride. It may feel quite strange at first, but the secret is to relax just enough to feel the rhythm of your pony's stride. Hold on to the saddle or mane until you feel safe, then take the reins. These are to control and guide your pony, not to hold you on.

As your pony walks, his head moves up and down. Hold the reins very lightly so that your hands can follow his rhythm. Sit well down in the saddle and try not to lean forward or look down.

The walk has four hoof beats. Each hoof strikes the ground separately in turn like this—near fore, off hind, off fore, near hind.

How a Pony Walks

Trotting

Trotting is more bouncy and may feel uncomfortable until you learn to rise. Do not try trotting until you have learned to walk. You can either sit down to trot or rise up and down in the saddle, in time with the pony's movements.

Rising to the trot is easy once you get it right. Let the bounce of your pony's stride push you up and forward a little from your knees. Then sit back gently into the saddle in a regular rhythm. Try to keep your hands and lower legs quite still. All this takes a lot of practice. It may help to say "Up-down" in time with your pony's stride at first. Lean slightly forward so you do not lose your balance. Keep your back straight but not stiff.

Your pony's legs move in pairs. The near fore leg and off hind leg together, then the off fore leg and near hind leg together. These are called diagonals.

How a Pony Trots

...ntering

...tering is exciting and is the ...ourite pace for most riders. ...member, though, it is quite ...ng, so practise for only a short ...e at first.

...egin with, hold the saddle ...n one hand. Sit up straight and ...w your hips to go with the ...vement of the pony, so your ...t stays in the saddle. You will be ...' at first and find it hard not to ...nce up and down. Your hands ...t hold the reins so your pony's ...d can swing up and down with ...stride.

...ony can canter with either fore ...leading. When cantering in a ...le, the inside leg should lead, ...n he will be properly balanced. ...canter has three hoof beats. ...en the off fore leg leads, as in ...picture, the hoof beats are near ...d, then off hind and near fore ...ether, and then off fore.

How a Pony Canters

...lloping

...e gallop is the fastest and most ...iting pace. You should gallop ...y if your pony is fit and you can ...trol him when cantering.

...ies increase their speed from ...ter to gallop by taking longer ...ides. They push harder with ...ir hind legs and stretch out their ...y, neck and head. Each foot is ...the ground for a shorter time, ...l there is a moment when all ...r feet are off the ground at once.

...ke your weight forward and right ...of the saddle to give your ...y's back the freedom to make ...extra effort. Have your weight ...your knees and feet. Never ...lop where there are people ...lking or where you might lose ...trol of your pony.

...in the canter, your pony's ...ide leg should lead if you are ...a bend. The gallop has four ...f beats. When the off fore leg ...ds, the hoof beats are—near ...d, off hind, near fore, off fore.

How a Pony Gallops

Aids

Every well-trained pony has been taught to understand a special set of signals from its rider. These signals are called aids. You must learn them so you can tell your pony what to do. Signals using your voice, hands, legs and body are called natural aids. Whips and spurs are artificial aids. You need quite a lot of practice to use these aids correctly. It is important that you learn on a trained po which understands and obeys Then you get the feel of doing things right.

Voice

Talk quietly but firmly. Your pony will learn to understand your tone and become confident, as long as you treat him well. Always keep your commands very simple. He will understand the sound of words such as "Walk" and "Trot" and "Whoa" but not long sentences.

Hands

Your hands help to control and guide your pony. Use your fingers to send messages along the reins telling him what to do. Never use the reins to hold you on. Try not to pull at your pony with the reins. This will make his mouth hard and he will soon begin to pay no attention when you tell him what to do.

Body

You can change the balance of your po by moving your body slightly. If you change the pressure of your seat on th saddle, he will soon learn to understan what you are telling him to do. The exercises at the bottom of the page an lots of practice on the lunge will help you to control your movements.

Legs

Use the lower part of your legs to tell your pony when to go fast Squeeze against his sides just behind the girth, using different amounts of pressure You control his hind-quarters by squeezin further back behind girth. This helps to te him when to move sideways or turn.

Exercises

It may seem difficult and tiring at first to ride the right way. This is because you are using muscles which do not often have to work. Try these exercises to help make you supple and fit. They are all great fun and will help to improve your riding. Practise for only a few minutes on a quiet pony somewhere safe, or with someone to hold your pony steady. Tie a knot in your reins so you do not catch your toe in them as you move about.

Rising in the Saddle

Lean slightly forward keeping your head up. Push down and raise your seat about 5 cms from the saddle. Then lower it gently. Hold your pony's mane at first if necessary.

Toe-Touching

Bend down and touch your toes like this. First one side then the other. Make sure your foot does not come up to meet your hand. Do not let your other leg slip backwards.

Swinging Arms

Swing round to face on side then the other, wit your arms at shoulder height. Do it in a smoot rhythm, keeping your legs quite still. Try arm circling too.

First Lessons

The girl in this picture is having a lesson on a lungeing rein. The instructor has control of the pony so she does not need to hold the reins. When you do this, you will really be able to feel your pony's movements. Hold on to the front of the saddle if you feel unsafe. A short lesson in each direction is enough, or your muscles become tired and stiff. It is important that you are lunged by someone experienced, and on a pony that goes well. Then you will be able to concentrate on keeping your balance and riding correctly.

Do not sit stiffly. Allow your body to move with the pony.

A lungeing cavesson is put on over the bridle. The rein must be at least 4.5 metres long. It has a swivel clip which is attached to a ring on the noseband.

On a left circle, the instructor holds the rein in his left hand and carries a whip in his right. His voice is usually enough to control the pony's speed.

Leaning Back

Lean forwards, from your waist. Then bend slowly backwards until you are lying on your pony's hindquarters. Do not let your legs slip forward.

2

Now return slowly to the correct position. Keep your arms folded all the time. This is difficult if you are not fit. It helps to make your back and stomach muscles strong.

1 Around the World

Swing your right leg over your pony's neck so you are sitting side saddle. Next swing your left leg, then your right leg, over his back so you are side saddle on the other side.

2

Lastly, swing your left leg over his neck to get you back where you started. Do this in a gentle rhythm, taking care not to kick your pony. Then try it going the other way.

Changing Pace

Changes from one pace to another should be smooth without any jerky movement. Make each signal clear and just strong enough for your pony to understand and obey. Watch a good rider on a well-trained horse. The aids are almost invisible and this is what you should aim for. It takes lots of practice and ca only be learned properly on a well-trained pony who will understand what you want it to do.

Increases of Pace

IF YOUR PONY TRIES TO MOVE BEFORE YOU GIVE THE SIGNAL, CHECK HIM BY INCREASING THE PRESSURE OF YOUR FINGERS ON THE REINS

KEEP YOUR HEAD UP

TRY NOT TO BECOME STIFF

LET YOUR HANDS FOLLOW THE MOVEMENTS OF HIS HEAD

KEEP A CONTAC WITH HIS MOUTH

Prepare to Walk

Walk On

As he sets off, lighten the contact on his mouth with your hands following the natural movement of his head. Don't lose contact completely or you will have no control.

Give a quick squeeze with the lower part of your legs and say "Walk on". As he sets off, slacken the reins so his head ca move in the rhythm of walk. Keep sitting up straight as he moves of

Decreases of Pace

TRY TO SIT STILL THEN YOU WILL NOT UNBALANCE YOUR PONY

WHEN YOU FEEL HIM RESPOND TO YOUR SIGNAL, RELAX YOUR FINGERS

USE YOUR LEGS TO KEEP HIM MOVING STRAIGHT AND STOP HIS HIND QUARTERS SWINGING OUT

TAKE CARE NOT 1 BOUNCE FORWAR, AND LOSE CONTROL

Canter to Trot

Trot to Walk

Straighten your back and press down with your seat. At the same time, increase your feel on the reins and say slowly. "Trot". Keep your legs close to his sides so he comes to a smooth well-balanced trot.

As before, sit to the trot and press your seat down. Gently resist with your hands as you say "Walk". Bring your legs again his sides to keep him going forward as he comes into a walk.

OR A SMOOTH CHANGE OF PACE
ROM WALK TO TROT, SIT THE FIRST
W STRIDES. START TO RISE
CE YOUR PONY IS TROTTING IN
STEADY RHYTHM

KEEP YOUR HEELS
LOW AND RISE FROM
YOUR KNEES

SIT DEEP IN THE
SADDLE AND PUSH
WITH YOUR SEAT

"ASK" WITH THE RIGHT REIN AND
GIVE FIRM PRESSURE WITH YOUR
LEFT LEG BEHIND THE GIRTH

USE YOUR INSIDE
LEG ON THE GIRTH
TO KEEP HIM GOING
FORWARD

DO EXACTLY THE
OPPOSITE TO
CANTER TO
THE LEFT

Trot

Canter

r pony will shorten his
slightly as he trots,
orten the reins
re squeezing with

your legs. Drive him
forward with your seat
and legs. Repeat the leg
pressure to keep up a
steady pace.

Sit deep into the saddle.
Use your inside leg on the
girth to keep him going
forward. Take the outside

leg back behind the girth.
Squeeze with the inside
rein to make him strike
off on the required rein.

NOT LET YOUR
SLIP FORWARD.
DOWN INTO
UR HEELS

REMEMBER YOU ARE GIVING
HIM A SIGNAL TO STOP — NOT
PULLING HIM TO A STANDSTILL

SAY "BACK" AND KEEP
HIM STRAIGHT WITH
YOUR LEGS

TWO OR THREE STEPS
ARE ENOUGH. THEN
MAKE HIM WALK
FORWARD

Halt

Rein Back

ighten your back and
ease your feel on the
s, saying "Whoa".
s with your legs to

bring his hind legs under
his body. This will bring
him to halt standing
square on all four legs.

This can only be done with
a well-trained pony. Keep
him standing straight
with his attention on you.

Give light leg aids, but
resist with your hands so
he steps backwards
instead of forwards.

23

Changing Direction

It is important to be able to ride your pony smoothly to right and left at each pace. You may find it harder to turn or circle one way than the other because he is stiff on one side. Exercises can help to make him supple.

Do not lean forward and pull him round. Sit well down in the saddle. Your seat and legs tell him what to do and your hands guide him. These pictures show how to turn right. Do exactly the opposite to turn left.

Turning to the Right

Sit up straight. Keep your seat square on the saddle or you will upset your pony's balance.

Your pony shoul[d] look to the right, bending his necl[k] not just by turni[ng] his head to the s[ide].

Hind feet should follow in the tracks of front feet.

How Ponies Bend their Spines

To turn or circle correctly, a pony should bend his neck and spine in the direction in which he is going. Seen from above, his body makes an arc, like this.

What Your Hands Do

Guide your pony by increasing pressure on the right rein. Give a little with your left hand to allow for the turn. But still keep enough contact to control him.

What Your Right Leg Does

The inside leg stays in the normal place close to the girth. Your pony should seem to bend himself round this leg as he turns. Keep up a steady pace.

What Your Left Leg Do[es]

This is the outside leg. Press it lightly against your pony's side further back than usual. This stops the hindquarters swinging out to the left.

...anging the Rein

...simply means turning and
...ng in another direction. Try to
...as smoothly as possible,
...out changing your pony's
...hm. To change from the left to
right rein, follow the blue line
on the menage plan below. Turn
diagonally across the school at
the first side marker after you
have ridden along the short side of
the school. When you reach the
marker diagonally across the
school, it is easy to change to the
right rein. You can also go
straight across. In a group, the
leading rider makes the change.

...hat is a Manege ?

...his is any enclosed area where you can
...ractise riding without being disturbed.

...n indoor riding school is ideal, but any
...at level area will do. You can use a
...iet corner of a field marked off with
...les of straw or oil cans. The usual size
...20 x 40 metres. Certain points round the
...anege are marked with letters. As these
...e always the same, it is a good idea to
...arn them by heart. Then you will know
...hat to do without looking when given
...instruction.

...xercises

...ide these exercises very thoroughly for
...egular short training periods. They
...ill help to make your pony supple and
...mprove your balance. Do them first at a
...alk, then a steady trot. Keep up the
...ame speed and rhythm. It is not easy
...o ride circles exactly. Large ones are
...asier, so start with these. Imagine that a
...ircle has been drawn on the ground.
...ook ahead and try to keep your pony on
...t. Next try a figure-of-eight, which is two
...ircles with a change of direction in the
...niddle. Lastly try a serpentine all the
...vay up the school.

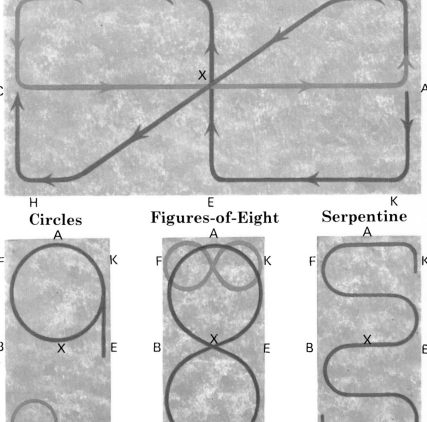

Circles **Figures-of-Eight** **Serpentine**

Learning to Jump

Jumping is great fun. But do not start until you feel secure and can control your pony at walk, trot and canter. It is a good idea to follow a plan of training, like the one below, with a teacher if possible.

Practice for short periods or your pony may get bored. Always finish when he has done something well. Have your stirrups a hole or two shorter to ride in the jumping position.

Approach

It is important to get the approach right, otherwise your pony will find it difficult to jump. Ride in the correct jumping position. Let your pony lower his head to judge the position and height of the jump

Take-Off

Make sure that you are not left behind as your pony pushes up and forward. Lean forward, but keep close to the saddle, and do not stand up in the stirrups. Move your hand forward to give him plenty of rein

Trotting Poles

This is a good way to start. It will help to improve your balance and make you more confident. Your pony will learn to adjust his stride, which is important for jumping. Use solid poles 10-15 cms in diameter and at least 3 metres long. Then your pony will really have to pick up his feet to trot over them. The second pony is following quite closely to encourage him. Once ponies know what to do, they should go one at a time.

Starting Off

Start by walking over one pole. Add more, one at a time, about 1.2 metres apart. Lean forward a little and keep a light feel on your pony's mouth.

A Line of Poles

Now try at a steady rising trot. Start with one pole and then add others as before. Trot over the middle of the poles, keeping up the same rhythm all the way.

Your First Jump

When you and your pony feel safe over trotting poles, place a low cavaletto about 2.4 metres from the last pole. Trot down the line and straight over the jump.

n the Air

still with your knees close to saddle. Try not to let your er legs slip backwards—then he not be unbalanced. He begins reach downwards with his front s after he has folded his hind s to clear the jump.

Landing

His head and neck come up to balance him as he lands. His front feet hit the ground hard. You can take some of the strain off his front legs by gently moving your shoulders and seat back just a little as you land.

Away

His front feet move off into the first stride as his hind feet come down almost in their place. Take control as soon as you land. The whole jump should be a smooth, flowing rhythm. You will find this much easier on an experienced pony.

avaletti

e Italian cavalry first ought of these. They nted fences they could ve easily and use to build ny different jumps. Now nost all riders use them train their horses. Work er Cavaletti will develop ur pony's muscles and in him to think calmly ut jumping. You can ctice your jumping sition and get the feel of ur pony's stride. Do not low the pony in front too sely.

low Cavaletti are Made

u can buy Cavaletti or make ur own. Make the cross-pieces th 75 cm lengths of wood 7 x 7 cm. en fix a pole or piece of timber etres long in between.

Other Cavaletti Jumps

You can make lots of different jumps with your Cavaletti. Make them low and easy to jump. Then your pony will enjoy it and not start the bad habit of refusing.

Cavaletti for Cantering

This needs quite a lot of skill. Use a pole and one Cavaletto first. Then add another about 2.8 metres away. Gradually build up a line of six jumps.

Rules for the Road

Here are some of the rules and signals you must know before riding on the road. These riders are all on the left because they live in a country, such as Australia or England, where the traffic drives on the left. If you live in a country, such as America, Germany, France, Italy or Holland, where the traffic drives on th right hand side of the road, then you must always ride o that side of the road too.

Riding on the Road
Do not ride on the road unless your pony is quiet in traffic. Keep him alert at a walk or slow trot so he will not slip or get out of control.

Turning
Signal clearly like this and in good time if you are going to turn left. Make the same signal with your right arm if you are going to turn right.

Stopping Traffic
Hold up your hand and look straight at the driver so he knows you mean him. Wait until you are sure the traffic has stopped before you cross.

I am going to st
Wave your outside ar up and down like this from the shoulder. Th tells drivers you are going to stop and asks passing traffic to slow down.

Riding in Groups
The first and last riders give signals. Ride this distance from the pony in front. Do not change pace without telling the others, or become separated from them.

"Thank You"
Thank everyone, with a nod or a smile, who is helpful. If the road is narrow and winding, go into a gateway or on to a grass verge to let traffic pass.

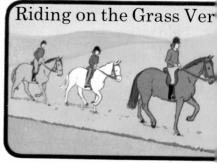
Riding on the Grass Ver
Ride on grass verges wherever possible, unless they are private or trimmed and mown. Never canter along a road verge. Your pony might shy into the traffic.

Leading Another Pony
Only lead another pony if you are experienced. Then have the led pony in a bridle on your inside, with his head level with your knee. This helps to control him.

Danger Ahead
Wait until the road is clear. Then ride firmly past the frightening object. Talk to your pony quietly and pat him to keep him calm. If he really plays up, get off.

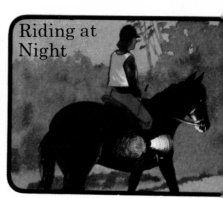
Riding at Night
If possible, do not ride at night or in a fog. If you must, always wear stirrup lights which shine white in front and red behind to warn other traffic you are there.

ountry Code

re are special unwritten s for people who ride in countryside. Always take a care of other people's and property. Remember you have a right to ride on roads, bridle paths and some other special areas. But all other fields, paths and woods are private. So always get permission first from the farmer or land owner. If you do this, behave sensibly and do no damage, you may be allowed to ride there again.

arting Off

Closing Gates

Keep to Field Edges

k that your pony is shod, that his tack fe and that it fits erly. Always wear a hat, sensible clothes plain shoes with a small heel. If you are going out riding alone, remember to tell someone where you are going and about how long you expect to be out.

Always remember to close gates that you have opened, even if the field seems empty. Teach your pony to help you do this.

Avoid damaging crops and fields, especially in wet weather. Be careful not to disturb livestock as you ride through fields.

iding Uphill

Riding Downhill

Where to Canter

n forward a little to leave pony's back and hind legs to push on up the hill. w him to stretch his neck n making the extra effort.

Keep your pony steady and lean forward a little to leave his back and hind quarters free. This will help him keep his balance.

Choose a quiet, slightly uphill path with soft ground, or the edge of a field if you can keep in control. Slow down to pass people on foot or other riders.

n a Long Trek

The Last Mile

Back Home

p for a rest of about half an r. Have a head collar over the le so you can take it off to let graze. Remove the saddle give him a short drink.

It is tempting to hurry home. But you should walk the last mile to bring your pony home cool and dry. Lead him if he is very tired or refuses to walk quietly.

A stabled pony must be rubbed down or walked until dry. If your pony is kept at grass, turn him out and he will rub himself down by having a good roll.

Popular Breeds of Ponies

The many different breeds of ponies have special qualities of size, strength and speed, which have developed over hundreds of years. Almost all are tough, gentle and quick to learn. This makes them ideal for children to ride.

There are many different types of this popular breed. Most make good riding ponies, being tough, calm, sure-footed quiet in traffic.

New Forest

Shetland

The smallest British breed at up to 1.1 metres. Shetland ponies can be any colour but black, brown and chestnut are the most usual. They are strong for their size and, if well trained, are specially good for small children to ride.

Pony of the Americas

This new breed was formed in 1956 by mating a Shetland stallion with an Appaloosa mare. The result was a very sma Appaloosa which has become popular in America as a child's pony. Usually they have white coats, peppered with spots coloured hair.

Fjord

These quiet ponies are becoming more popular outside their native country of Norway. They are easy to spot by their dun colour with black legs and black hairs in their manes and tails. They make good steady ponies to ride and drive, being tough, easy to feed and very good natured.

Iceland

These tough little ponies of under 13 hands were brought to Iceland in the 9th century. Some work as pack ponies. Others, which a ridden, learn a special pace which is half-w half-trot.

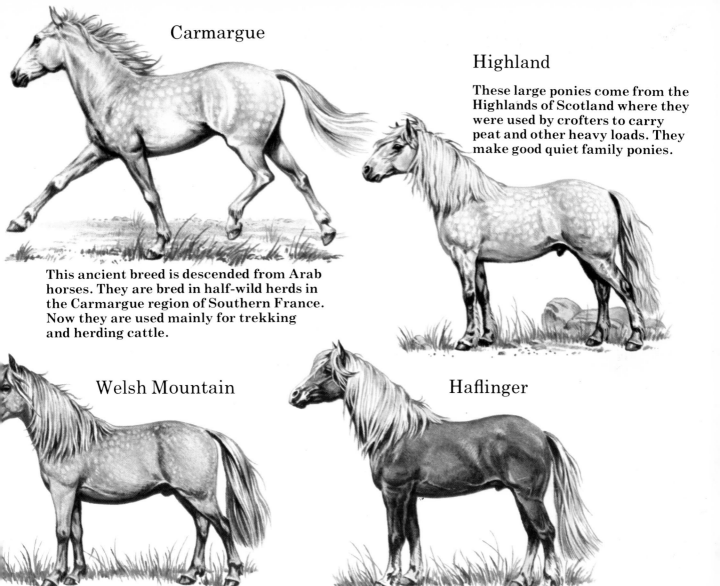

Carmargue

This ancient breed is descended from Arab horses. They are bred in half-wild herds in the Carmargue region of Southern France. Now they are used mainly for trekking and herding cattle.

Highland

These large ponies come from the Highlands of Scotland where they were used by crofters to carry peat and other heavy loads. They make good quiet family ponies.

Welsh Mountain

e beautiful ponies, with flowing manes
ails, have lived in Wales since Roman
s. They are popular all over the world for
g, driving and breeding, being good
red, strong and nimble.

Haflinger

All Haflinger ponies can be traced back to one chestnut stallion called Folie, born in Austria in 1874. They are tough, sure-footed ponies and used to living in mountains. They are now popular in many countries

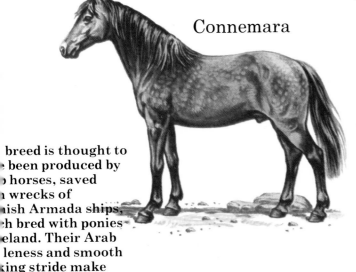

Connemara

breed is thought to
been produced by
horses, saved
wrecks of
ish Armada ships,
h bred with ponies
eland. Their Arab
leness and smooth
king stride make
n ideal family
es.

Exmoor

These ponies with light coloured muzzles still live in half-wild herds on Exmoor. They are only about 12.3 hands high, but are sure-footed, have a smooth flat trot and are fast and good at jumping.

Index

aids.	20-21, 22-23
bits,	5
blacksmith	6, 14-15
breeds of ponies	30-31
bridles	4-5
cleaning	4-5
fitting	5
parts of	5
removing	5
Cavaletti	27
cantering	19, 23
catching ponies	2-3
colours, pony	3
country code	29
dismounting	17
exercises	20-21, 25
feeding	6, 8-9, 10-11
fences.	8-9
first-aid kit	13
galloping	19
gates	8, 29
girths	4, 5, 16
grass	6, 8, 10
grazing	6, 8, 9, 10
grooming	6, 9, 12
hands (measurement)	2
hay	6, 8, 10
headcollar	2, 3
health	13
hooves	12, 14, 15
horse shoes	6, 14-15
illnesses, common pony	13
jumping	7, 26-27
Cavaletti	27
jumps	26-27
lungeing	21
markings, pony,	2
manege	25
mounting	16-17
mucking out	10, 11
paces,	18-19
changing	22-23
points of horse	2-3
poisonous plants	9
ponies,	
aids	20-21
breeds of	30-31
catching	2
colours	3
choosing	6-7
feeding	6, 8-9, 10-11
fencing	8
grooming	6, 9, 13
health	13
illnesses	13
leading	3
markings	2
measuring	2
paces	18-19
shoeing	14-15
stabling	8, 10, 11
reins	16, 17, 18, 19, 20, 21, 24,
lungeing	
roads, riding on	
rugging up	
rugs,	6, 9,
saddles,	
cleaning	
girths	4,
jumping	
parts of	
putting on	
removing	
sitting in	18
saddling up	
shelters,	8, 10,
shoes, horse	6, 14-
signals (aids),	20
road	
spurs	
stables,	8, 10,
cleaning	
routine	
tools	
stirrups	4, 16, 17,
tack	4-5, 6,
trotting,	18, 22-
poles	
vets (veterinary surgeons)	6, 7,
walking	18,
water	
whips	20,
worms	6, 8,

Telling a Pony's Age

This pony is under two years old. His bones are soft and he is still growing, so his rump may be higher than his withers. He is alert and interested in everything.

A mature pony of about eight years is in the prime of his life. He looks proud and confident, and is well-muscled and strong. Hollows over his eyes may begin to show.

This pony is nearly 30. He looks thin and bony. His muscles are slack and he may not eat well. T hollows over his eyes are deep a his movements have become sti

First published in 1978
Usborne Publishing Ltd
20 Garrick Street
London WC2E 9BJ

Published in Australia by Rigby Ltd, Adelaide, Sydney, Melbourne, Brisbane, Perth.

Published in Canada by Hayes Publishing Ltd. Burlington, Ontario.

Printed in Belgium b Henri Proost, Turnh Belgium.